Humpback Whales

ABDO
Publishing Company

A Buddy Book
by
Julie Murray

VISIT US AT
www.abdopub.com

Published by Buddy Books, an imprint of ABDO Publishing Company, 4940 Viking Drive, Suite 622, Edina, Minnesota 55435. Copyright © 2003 by Abdo Consulting Group, Inc. International copyrights reserved in all countries. No part of this book may be reproduced in any form without written permission from the publisher.

Printed in the United States.

Edited by: Christy DeVillier
Contributing Editors: Matt Ray, Michael P. Goecke
Graphic Design: Maria Hosley
Image Research: Deborah Coldiron
Cover Photograph: NOAA (National Oceanic & Atmospheric Administration)
Interior Photographs: Minden Pictures, NOAA

Library of Congress Cataloging-in-Publication Data

Murray, Julie, 1969-
   Humpback whales / Julie Murray.
      p. cm. — (Animal kingdom)
   Summary: Introduces the habitat and characteristics of the humpback whale.
   ISBN 1-57765-708-X
      1. Humpback whale—Juvenile literature. [1. Humpback whale. 2. Whales.] I. Title. II. Animal kingdom (Edina, Minn.)

QL737.C424 M87 2002
599.5'25—dc21

                                                                    2001045857

Contents

Sea Mammals

What do whales, dolphins, and porpoises have in common? These animals are **cetaceans**. Cetaceans are **mammals** that live in the water. Sea lions, walruses, and seals are sea mammals, too.

Some **mammals** that live on land are elephants, apes, dogs, and mice. These land mammals do not look like whales and other sea mammals. Yet, all mammals have some things in common. Mammals breathe with lungs instead of gills. Mammals are born alive instead of hatching from eggs. Baby mammals drink their mother's milk. People are mammals, too.

Humpback Whales

A hump is like a big, round bump. Do humpback whales have humped backs? No. It only looks like humpbacks have humped backs when they dive. Yet, this is how the humpback whale got its name.

Humpback whales do not have humped backs.

Flipper

Pleats

Flipper

Humbacks belong to a special group of whales. This group is the rorqual whales. Rorquals are the only whales with special **pleats**. These pleats are on the underside of the rorqual whale. Feeding rorquals will stretch these pleats to make their mouths bigger.

What They Look Like

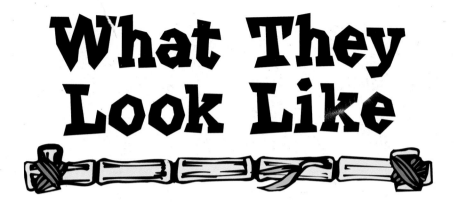

Humpback whales are huge! An adult humpback may weigh about 29 tons (26 t). These whales can grow over 45 feet (14 m) long. The female humpback is bigger than the male.

A humpback's fluked tail.

The humpback whale's giant head has many large bumps, or tubercles. The humpback's two big **flippers** can grow over 15 feet (5 m) long. Its tail has two parts, or flukes, that jut out sideways. Bumps and marks on the flukes are different for each humpback.

All whales have **blowholes**. The humpback has two blowholes on top of its head. Whales take in air and let it out through their blowholes. Only a tiny bit of water leaks into the blowhole. A whale sprays out this water when it blows out air. This watery spray is a sign that a whale is "blowing."

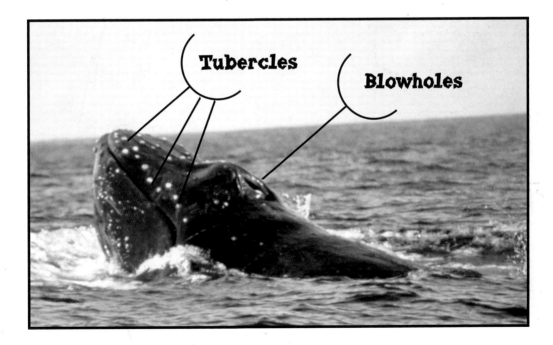

Tubercles

Blowholes

Where They Live

Humpback whales swim in all oceans of the world. These **migrating mammals** swim to different places when the seasons change. Humpbacks spend their summers in cool waters. They migrate to warmer waters for the winter. A humpback's migrating trip may take 30 or 40 days.

Singers of the Sea

Male humpback whales will sing when they are in warm waters. Other male humpbacks in the area join in singing the same song. One song can last 20 minutes. Humpbacks may sing for a few hours or a few days. The humpback's song slowly changes year by year.

Eating

Humpback whales can eat over 3,000 pounds (1,361 kg) of **plankton** each day. Humpbacks also gulp down large schools, or groups, of small fish.

Humpback whales have baleen instead of teeth.

Humpback whales have **baleen** plates instead of teeth. Baleen plates are long and thin. They hang inside the humpback's mouth. Baleen helps humpbacks catch food. Humpbacks feed by gulping a lot of fish-filled water. The water escapes easily. But the fish stay trapped among the baleen plates.

Bubble Nets

Humpback whales make bubbles to trap their food. These whales dive down below fish. Then, they swim up and around the fish, making bubbles. This "net" of bubbles traps the tiny fish. Humpbacks are the only whales that make these special bubble nets.

17

Breaching

Dolphins, humpback whales, and other whales breach. A breaching whale leaps from the water. Then, it falls back down making a big splash.

A breaching humpback.

People love to watch humpbacks breach.

Humpbacks may breach for different reasons. A humpback may breach to get rid of small pests living on its skin. Maybe breaching is how whales "show off" to other whales. Maybe whales breach to warn others of danger. A breaching whale calf is probably just playing.

Humpback Calves

Female humpback whales have one baby every two or three years. Whale babies are called calves.

A mother humpback with her calf.

Newborn humpback calves can swim right away.

A newborn humpback calf is about 13 feet (4 m) long. It may weigh over two tons (1,814 kg). A calf will drink its mother's milk and quickly grow bigger. At one year old, a young whale can live on its own. This whale may live for another 40 years.

Important Words

baleen long, thin plates that hang inside the humpback whale's mouth.

blowhole the opening on top of a whale that is used for taking in air.

cetacean a water mammal that has flippers, a tail, and one or two blowholes.

flipper a flat, paddle-shaped body part that cetaceans use for swimming.

mammal most living things that belong to this special group have hair, give birth to live babies, and make milk to feed their babies.

migrate to move from one place to another as the seasons change.

plankton tiny plants and animals floating in the water.

pleats special folds that can open and close.

Web Sites

The Whale Center of New England

www.whalecenter.org
This site features whale sounds, pictures, and ways to help endangered whales.

Nature: Humpback Whales

www.pbs.org/wnet/nature/humpback
How do scientists study humpbacks? Why do these cetaceans sing? Find out here.

Humpback Whale

www.zoomdinosaurs.com/subjects/whales/species/Humpbackwhale.shtml
Facts, fun activities, and links to other humpback whale sites can be found here.

Index